MW00676211

VROOMANS NOSE

VROOMANS NOSE

SKY ISLAND OF THE SCHOHARIE VALLEY

A STUDY BY

VINCENT J. SCHAEFER

PURPLE MOUNTAIN PRESS

Fleischmanns, New York

First Edition, 1992
published by
Purple Mountain Press, Ltd.
Main Street, P.O. Box E3
Fleischmanns, New York 12430-0378

Copyright © 1992 by Vincent J. Schaefer

All rights reserved. No part of this publication may be reproduced
or transmitted in any form or by any electronic or mechanical means
including information storage and retrieval systems without permission
in writing from the publisher, except by a reviewer who wishes to quote
brief passages in connection with a review written for inclusion in a
magazine, newspaper or broadcast.

Library of Congress Cataloging-in-Publication Data

Schaefer, Vincent J.
  Vroomans Nose : sky island of the Schoharie Valley : a study / by
Vincent J. Schaefer. -- 1st ed.
     p.   cm.
  ISBN 0-935796-35-5 (pbk.)
  1. Schoharie Creek Valley (N.Y.)--History. 2. Vromans Nose (N.Y.)
3. Geology--New York (State)--Schoharie Creek Valley. I. Title.
F127.S3S27   1992
974.7'45--dc20   92-37191
                                                          CIP

Second Printing 1993

Manufactured in the United States of America

Contents

Foreword

FOR MANY YEARS people have traveled to the Schoharie Valley to view its natural beauty and to climb the mountain, known as Vroomans Nose, upon which one's eye cannot help but focus. The mountain is different and is separated from all others which surround it. The questions regarding this landmark formation are many, and interest has always been high as described in articles from unknown newspapers, perhaps including the *Middleburgh Gazette* and the *Middleburgh News*. Several columns were written about an "excursion" to the Schoharie Valley by the Dana Natural History Society of Albany and "its friends of Albany Institute and of the Nature Club, and of the Troy Scientific Association." The article states that it was a lovely Saturday morning, June 1st but the year was unrecorded. Since the Hon. Peter Swart Danforth's home was placed at the visitors' disposal and George L. Danforth acted as the guide who hosted the occasion, it must have been the latter half of the nineteenth century.

The visitors had traveled by rail and their number "hardly half filled the elegant, new, commodious car which, by the kindness of the Delaware and Hudson Canal Company, had been furnished for the excursion." After a "very hearty welcome address" by Mr. George Danforth, "the company took their places in the carriages and omnibuses which were awaiting them and were given a most delightful drive to the Onistagrawa mountain — two miles distant from the village. The view of the projecting cliff, towering to an elevation of 600 feet above and almost overhanging at one point the roadway, was grand and scarcely surpassed by that from the summit. The ascent being somewhat tedious, it was not undertaken. Halting by the roadside to drink some of the sparkling water from the mountain mineral spring, the company retraced their eyes upon the beauty of the surrounding mountains."

In another place it is stated that they "contemplated the facsimile of Mr. Vrooman's nose in solemn awe, and came to the conclusion that he must have lived in an age when special attention was given to the development of nasal organ."

Today we do not travel in carriages, but we can climb the Nose, learn about its formation, the history and the inhabitants, and enjoy the great natural beauty of the area. Although he has long had an affection for Vroomans Nose and its environs and a desire to share his great knowledge, Dr. Schaefer only began formally compiling this material in 1984. Now with some editing, added stories and photographs, the book is complete.

Please note that the name "Vrooman" or "Vroman" appears in Dr. Schaefer's original manuscript with two "oo's." Many of the descendants of Adam Vrooman use only one "o". Vromans Nose Preservation Society was incorporated with one "o." Occasionally, both forms are found in the same original documents. It may be noted also that the possessive apostrophe has been dropped as we speak of the common title "Vroomans Nose."

Those who know the Nose intimately will notice that the picture on the back cover was inadvertantly reversed.

Helene S. Farrell
Historian, Photographer

Acknowledgments

IN THE PREPARATION of this book I want to thank Mrs. Helene Farrell, daughter of an old friend of mine, who took a deep personal interest in its production. All of the photographs in the book are hers unless otherwise noted.

Dr. Robert Titus of Hartwick College, Oneonta, was kind enough to review the chapters on geology, and Dr. Michael Kudish of Paul Smith's College provided a preliminary, yet thorough, list of flora printed as Appendix C.

Also I want to cite Wallace Van Houten whose devoted interest to Vroomans Nose and active protective action in making the terrain available to its many visitors, is legendary.

Also, my old friend, George Cooley, who during the final days of the fund drive for the purchase of the Nose provided the monetary gift which elicited matching funds that assured the property could be purchased.

The main funds were provided by three sisters, direct descendants of Adam Vrooman: Mrs. Terri V. Hartmann, Mrs. Susan V. Walker, Mrs. Margaret V. Nowak, and Harold B. Vroman. Without their vision and sense of

history and stewardship, it is unlikely that the Vromans
Nose Preservation Corporation could have been formed
and that this unique and beautiful place would have been
provided and protected for posterity.

Finally, I want to pay tribute to Harold B. Vroman,
historian, visionary and doer who solved the many
problems that arose in the acquisition and dedication of
the Nose and which were finally overcome by his persistence and perseverance.

Vincent J. Schaefer, Sc.D.

Vroomans Nose*

THE SCHOHARIE VALLEY is one of the most beautiful regions in our country. Settled by German Palatines and some Dutch pioneers from Schenectady, the valley has harbored farming communities for more than 275 years. The highly productive soils that cover the extensive flats bordering the Schoharie River have been used to produce food from the area's earliest occupation in prehistoric times, to the period of colonial migration from the Hudson and Mohawk Valleys, and through the present.

Some of the finest fertile land comprising more than 1200 acres occupies the broad flats west and southwest of Middleburgh. This was purchased from the resident Native Ameircans in 1712 by the Dutch pioneer, Adam Vrooman of Schenectady. Along the northern edge of this rich flatland a unique natural mountain called by the Native Americans, "Onistagrawa" (Corn Mountain), rises abruptly some 600 feet in the form of a vertical cliff having aprons of fallen rock on the south and eastern sides. The

*The Nose is 1,230 feet MSL, and its highest point is at 42 35' 30" north latitude and 74 21' 30" west longitude. The elevation of the nearby Schoharie River is 630 feet.

northern slope is more gentle, while to the west the rocky summit drops a hundred feet or so to reach a narrow neck of land which extends westerly for a half mile, rising again to become part of the mountainous western highland of the valley. Thus the Nose becomes a rocky island in the region.

This geographic structure is unique to the surrounding countryside as the only east-west trending cliff of the entire valley. Its existence is probably due to the fact that when the great continental glacier invaded the valley, it was moving in a westerly direction through the upper valley of the Norman's Kill and across the Helderberg Plateau. The summit of the Nose was protected by a tough cap rock of Hamilton sandstone which was polished by stone embedded in the base of the moving glacier. The striations produced show that the glacier's direction was 10° south of due west.

From every direction the tree-fringed summit of Vroomans Nose, as Onistagrawa came to be called after Adam Vrooman and his sons established Vroomansland, presents a striking presence. The natural nose-like profile, which has existed for more than a hundred centuries following the melting of the great glacier, will remain undefiled by man-made structures into the foreseeable future. Purchased in 1983, through the combined efforts of the Schoharie County Historical Society, several descendants of the original settlers and an amalgam of public-spirited citizens, the Nose has been dedicated to a "forever wild" category. Its summit has been made available to visitors who wish to climb it, where they can enjoy the remarkable views from the edge of the south-facing cliff top.

Vroomans Nose from the cemetery. Winter, 1985

Geology

THE ROCKS that form Vroomans Nose have been classified as representative of the middle of the Devonian System. Devonian rocks are the most widespread of any of the deposits within the bounds of New York State, covering nearly a third of its total area. They have a combined thickness of between 8,000 and 9,000 feet, although in the Schoharie Valley the Devonian thickness is less than 2,000.

Originally these rocks probably extended north to the southern Adirondacks and east into Massachusetts. The easterly boundary now forms the Helderberg Escarpment about 15 miles west of the Hudson River. This contains remnants of the Upper Silurian, the Lower and the earlier phases of the Middle Devonian. The latter constitutes Vroomans Nose.

While the lower rocks of the Devonian in eastern New York are limestones ranging from the Upper Manlius to the Schoharie Grit and the Onondaga Limestone, the bulk of the Devonian consists of sandstones, shales and the coarser sands and pebbles of the Catskill Mountains.

The Upper Devonian beds include the massive sediments which form the Catskill Mountains and which consist of coarse sands and multicolored pebbles. They extend westward as far as Indiana.

Restoration exhibit of the Gilboa Forest in the State Museum
during 1930s. Labeled: "Oldest Known Fossil Forest."
Photo by James Glenn

The lower part of this Upper Devonian bed includes the famous "Gilboa Tree" (a giant seed fern) which was discovered in 1869 when an autumn freshet uncovered standing stumps of fossil trees in the bed along the Schoharie Creek. The greatest amount of study was done by Winifred Goldring, associate paleontologist, New York State Museum, when the dam for the Schoharie (Gilboa) Reservoir was under construction from 1917-1926. The Gilboa Tree occupies the same niche as the "Naples Tree" (a giant club moss) which is in the same formation and is located at the southern end of Canandaigua Lake, southeast of Rochester.

At first glance, the imposing south-facing cliff of Vroomans Nose appears to be varieties of grayish-brown rock ranging from massive layers of dense rock to friable layers in between the more solid portions. The cliff is the sedimentary rock of an ancient sea. Some layers contain the remnants of invertebrate life in the form of fossil shells, corals, and other occupants of the sea. Other layers have little or no such remains, but they all belong to the Middle Devonian.

The deposit lies in what geologists have termed the "Hamilton Beds" of the Middle Devonian System — having an age of nearly 400 million years. This is basically a rich, fossiliferous fauna containing more than 800 species in total variety with at least 300 common species throughout the deposit across the state. These are mostly shells although they contain sponges, corals, crinoids and starfish.

The summit rock of Vroomans Nose is a particularly dense, fairly hard, thick layer which resisted the scouring action of the continental glacier that approached the Nose eastwards from the Helderberg plateau, polishing and scratching the surface but not breaking it in any way except for the chatter marks. These marks show the passage of large boulders embedded at the bottom of the moving ice as it flowed in a westerly direction (10° south of west).

Cobbles from the Hamilton beds were transported from the eastern side of the Nose and the hills to the east of Middleburgh and dropped below the face of the cliff to form the talus slopes 300 to 600 feet below the summit rock.

Similar horizontal layers of the same rock that forms Vroomans Nose occur to the west and are particularly well exposed in the valley of Panther Creek which culminates

Striation and chatter marks on Summit Rock.

at Boucks Falls. These rock layers also comprise "The Cliff" which rises abruptly to the northeast of the village of Middleburgh, and in the mid-section of the mountains lining the sides of the Schoharie River and the Little Schoharie which enters the main stream just south of Middleburgh.

No trace of the harder crystalline basement rocks of the Adirondacks to the north can be found in the Schoharie Valley except in the glacial drift. These occur as cobblestones and boulders embedded in the clayey glacial till that is found on the east-facing slope of the valley and in

the stream beds of the Schoharie tributaries which flow
from east and west into the river.

4—Onistagrawa Mountain, Middleburg, N. Y.

Post card view of Summit Rock from Fultonham Road
(NYS Route 30).

Schoharie Valley Fossils

THE SCHOHARIE VALLEY is the locality where the first systematic and successful effort was made to classify the sedimentary rocks of New York State. This landmark action was the work of the John Gebhards — father and son — early in the 1800s. They were naturalists of the "old school," with a special flair for paleontology. Together they combed the ledges, cliffs, old stone walls and early quarries and assembled their fossil finds with relation to the specific strata which contained them. Their collecting grounds included the main Schoharie and its tributaries extending from the Mohawk River southward to Gilboa and beyond.

They were successful in establishing the characteristics and fossil remains of the successive layers of sedimentary shales, sandstones and limestones in the Schoharie Valley which spanned a geologic period of a hundred million years. These periods ranged from what is called the upper Ordovicain through the Silurian and on through the lower, middle and upper Devonian.

In 1836, Lieutenant William Mather, who was assigned to develop a report of the first Geologic District of New

York as part of the Natural History Survey of the state, sought the services, expertise and knowledge of John Gebhard, Jr. This ambitious survey was supported by an "Act of the State Legislature" and resulted in a remarkable series of publications about New York State; it also

John Gebhard, Jr.
New York State Geologist, 1841

led to the start of the New York State Museum in Albany. The proximity of the Schoharie Valley to Albany was very fortunate and scientists from many parts of the world became acquainted with the unusually fine series of deposits which were so easy to visit.

More than fifty years ago I was asked by the director of the Schenectady Museum to evaluate a fossil collection which was offered for sale by the owners of the Gebhard homestead. Although at the time I was not aware of the historical importance of this collection, I urged Director Jones to acquire it if at all possible. This was done in cooperation with the New York State Museum in Albany, which took some of the smaller specimens in the collection. The John Gebhard collection of Schoharie Valley fossils comprises the major paleontological collection at the Schenectady Museum.

While we have not yet searched this collection to determine whether or not the Gebhard collection contains samples from the Hamilton shales and sandstones of Vrooman's Nose, I am confident that most, if not all, of the type specimens of the Vrooman's Nose strata are represented in the collection. Eventually, I hope it will be possible to assemble a representative fossil collection from the outcroppings of Vrooman's Nose to be located at the Old Stone Fort Museum at Schoharie.

In passing, it should be pointed out that a short distance below the bridge spanning the Schoharie River at Schoharie near the Gebhard homestead is a small cavern called Gebhard's or Clark's Cave. I explored it about 40 years ago shortly after the tooth of a ground sloth had been found in it. Dr. Caryl Haskins, later president of the Carnegie Institution, was the leader of our little expedition. I took the lead in the cave and found it necessary to inch forward on my stomach through a very tight channel, immersed in a combination of mud and running water. The cavern widened somewhat but then narrowed again until progress was blocked by a pillar of calcium carbonate. My light showed that an extension of the cave

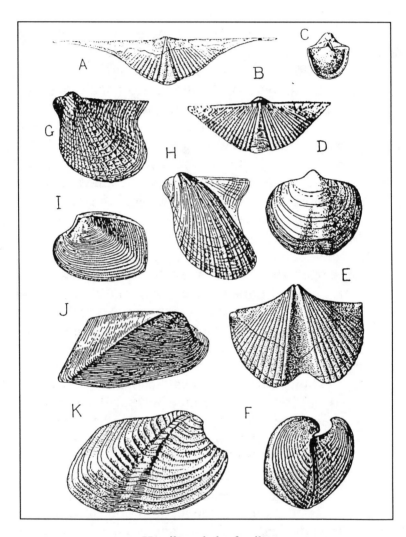

Hamilton shales fossils.
(Brachiopods, A-F; pelecypods, G-K.) A, B *Spirifer mucronatus*, x-3/4.
C *Ambocoelia umbonata*. D *Athyris spiriferoides*, x-3/4. E, F *Spirifer granulosus*, x-3/4. G *Actinopteria boydi*, x-34. H *Pterinea flabellum*, x-3/4. K *Grammysia bisulcata*, x-3/4.

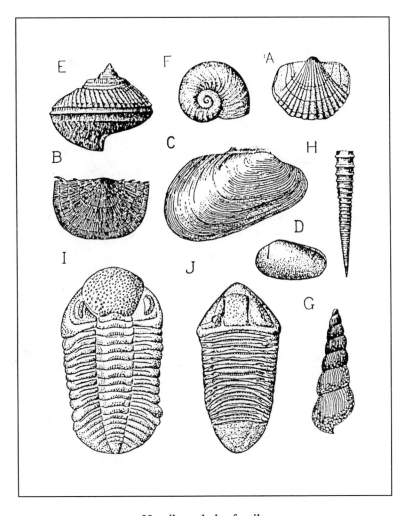

Hamilton shales fossils.
(Brachiopods, A, B; pelecypods C,D; gastrodods, E-G; pteropod, H; trilobites, I, J.) A *Tropidoleptus carinatus*, x-3/4. B *Chonetes cronatus*. C *Modiomorpha mytiloides*. D *Nuculites oblongatus*, x-3/4. E *Bembexia sulcomarginata*, x-3/4. F *Diaphorostoma lineatum*, x-3/4. G *Loxonema hamiltoniae*. H *Tentaculites bellulus*, x2. I *Phacops rana*, x-1/2. J *Homalonotus (Dipleura) dekayi*, x-3/8.

continued, but the pillar was so massive as to prevent any further exploration. Our clothes were so plastered with mud that upon leaving the cave we went to the Schoharie Creek nearby, lay in the water and attempted to wash the mud from our clothes, but without much success. Memory fails to provide further details.

Note might be made of John Gebhard's association with Thomas Cole, the Hudson Valley artist. It is believed that the inspiration for the caverns in Cole's four large oil paintings, "Voyage Through Life," was gained through his experience with Gebhard in Ball's (also known as Knoepfel's Cave, today Gage's Cave) and Gebhard's Caves in Schoharie County.

Effect of the Glacier

DURING THE LAST great ice age when a mile-thick glacier moved from the north into New York State covering all the land including the high peaks of the Adirondacks, a very large lobe of ice flowed southward down the Champlain and Hudson Valleys. Somewhere south of Glens Falls a side lobe spread westerly up the Mohawk Valley and across the Mariaville and Helder hills (foothills of the Helderbergs) into the Schoharie Valley.

The rocks on the bottom of this slowly moving mass of ice ground and polished the tough and resistant rock of the Hamilton formation which comprises the present summit of Vrooman's Nose. The grinding and polishing effect of the rocks in the base of the glacier produced the glacial scratches, striae and chatter marks that are still visible there.

These glacial effects are beautifully exposed on the southwestern end of the cap rock of the Nose where the thin cover of soil and humus was stripped away a century or more ago to provide the "dance floor" that exists there at the present time. I do not know when this was done. However, this flat expanse of rock has been used for more than a hundred years as a register, many of the visitors inscribing artistic names, dates and/or initials.

Unfortunately, in recent years, thoughtless individuals have used the spray can to paint their affiliations. When compared to the earlier graffitti, this action does not

Inscriptions in the "dance floor."

reflect favorably on the perpetrators. The first date found probably represents the time when the dance floor was established, since there is a certain element among the human species who can't resist putting their name or initials on a portion of a large surface. The building of fires on this surface has also caused splitting and breaking of the shale, leading to deterioration.

Further evidence of local glaciation is not easy to establish. Talus slopes on the south and southwestern slopes are presently covered with vegetation. The southeastern side, which is part of the Commons area (see page 62), has a large barrow region where the talus slope has been partially removed. That area might be expected to contain some glacial debris, but if it was present, it has been trucked away.

The "dance floor."

An examination of the mountain slopes and drainage streams at the end of Vroomansland west of Watsonville and Fultonham provides evidence of glacial deposits. Along Hardscrabble Road west of Watsonville the steep slopes bordering the road are cut into glacial till, a very dense conglomeration of hard clay and glacial boulders, cobbles and pebbles. Among the rounded and polished pebbles and cobblestone are sandstone and limestone characteristic of the bedrock east and northeast of Vroomans Nose comprising the Helderhills and the Schoharie and Duanesburg Hills. However, I found fine examples of Adirondack rocks including garnet-bearing gneiss, granite and Potsdam sandstone in the till along the road.

Similarly, in the creek bed of the stream which flows out of the hills west of Fultonham, I observed many fossiliferous rocks from the nearby limestone and sandstone strata, along with some very large boulders and cobblestones of Adirondack type rocks, similar to those found along Hardscrabble Road. These rocks from the Adirondacks are identical to those I have found near Schenectady in the gravels along the Mohawk River also of glacial origin from the Adirondacks.

Natural History

THE TREES, SHRUBS, FLOWERS, ferns, mosses, lichens, birds, animals and insects of Vroomans Nose fit the pattern that pervades most of the Helderberg Plateau and the Schoharie Valley Mountains. While these sedimentary rocks are related to the Catskill Mountains, the thin soils covering them were left mostly by the glacier some 10,000 years ago.

The dominant trees of the Nose are the white pine and hemlock, which are represented examples well over 100 years old, scattered along the steep northern slopes. The summit trees include chestnut, oak, red cedar, several species of hickory, white ash and shad blow.

Large patches of bearberry and huckleberry are spread across the thin soil, which covers the glacially grooved and scratched summit rock with smaller patches of rock saxifrage and fringed polygala.

Large chunks of stratified rock covered with mosses and ferns are scattered at different levels on the north slope. The common polypody is the most frequently seen rock fern, although a few, like the maidenhair spleenwort, can be found. Large patches of the lichen called rock tripe

31

occur on the cliff facing on the southeastern end of the Nose.

The strong thermals which characterize the air above the southern cliff face develop as soon as it becomes heated by the sun. These thermals are used by a host of soaring birds, particularly turkey vultures. I have seen more than a score of them perched along the cliff edge seemingly taking turns at leaping off the cliff into the thermals and soaring upward until they are no longer visible, after which in long swooping dives they return to their cliff-edge perch. Feathers of smaller birds are frequently found along the cliff edge, indicating that they have fallen prey to the various hawks which frequent the region.

The thermals rising along the south-facing slope also carry insects, including a variety of butterflies, upward to the summit. On some of the terraces of the north slope large anthills exist. Whether they are built by the species which build huge mounds six to eight feet in diameter and three to four feet high remains to be seen. Several colonies exist which are producing large hills, but they have not as yet produced the giant size seen on a terrace of the mountain north of Line Creek. A unique species of spiders was identified here in the late 1930s by Dr. Sherman Bishop of the University of Rochester.

Of the animals, mostly deer have left traces this year (1985). These are in the form of well worn trails with tracks in muddy areas. Squirrel nests are abundant in the trees.

A checklist of flora of Vroomans Nose, compiled by Dr. Michael Kudish, comprises Appendix C.

Early Inhabitants

It is likely that Paleo Indians visited the Schoharie Valley not long after the great Continental Glacier began to disappear. The nearest camp of these ancient people is near Athens along the Hudson River about 20 miles east of Vroomans Nose. A natural route from the Hudson to the Schoharie Valley would follow Catskill Creek to its source, thence down the deep valley to the Little Schoharie and thus to the great flats of Vroomansland under the brow of the Nose. An alternate route (today NYS Route 145), would follow the northern slopes of the Catskill Mountains or the valleys of the Hannacroix, the Onesquethaw and the other streams that flow toward the Hudson.

There is much evidence of the camps and villages of the successors to the Paleo Indians. This evidence appears in the form of chipped flint, dark organic middens and in the later period as plain and decorated clay pot fragments. The earlier non-ceramic occupations occurred mostly on small terraces, particularly in the region where the Little Schoharie joined the Schoharie and along the two streams which flowed from the north and south sides of Vroomans Nose.

Near the northerly stream (called Line Creek, since it is the dividing line marking the boundary of the Towns of Middleburgh and Fulton) is a place called Wilders Hoek, where an historic village of the Schoharie Indians was located.

Evidence of Native American campsites exists on the summit of Vroomans Nose in the form of flint chippings, broken arrowheads and fire-cracked stone. These remains appear to have been left by the same people who occupied the terraces on the flats below. The materials used for making projectile points, arrowheads, scrapers, knives, and other chipped stone for making artifacts included a fairly good grade of flint. This was the type found as lenses in the Onondaga limestone and which occur as large workshop sites on the hilltops east of the upper Susquehanna River near Oneonta. There was an immense quarry at Flint Mine Hill near West Coxsackie and smaller deposits were found along the edges of the flat plateau of the Big and Little Nose Mountains, on either side of the Mohawk River at Fort Hunter. This latter flint is quite distinctive, ranging from white to grey and yellow. These different sources of artifact material suggest active trading, exploration, and travel by the prehistoric settlers of the Vroomans Nose area.

When we consider the historic period of occupancy of the Schoharie region, especially near Vroomans Nose, an extremely interesting relationship emerges. Although there were considerable tension and trouble between the German Palatines, led by John Conrad Weiser, and the Dutch settlers (mostly of the Vrooman family from Schenectady), there is evidence of tolerance between the

Mohegans of the Hudson Valley, the Schoharie Indians, the Dutch settlers and the Mohawks of the mid-Mohawk Valley (above Amsterdam).

The eastern boundary of the Mohawk-Iroquois was the steep, rocky projection southwest of Wolf Hollow about midway between Schenectady and Amsterdam. No Mohawk villages are known east of that rocky eminence. Its Indian name — Kina-quar-i-ones — is said to mean "The Rock that Marks the Boundary of the Mohawk's Country."

The deed received by Adam Vrooman from the Indians and a subsequent deed given by him to his son, Jan Vrooman, recognizes the occupancy of the Schoharie Indian village near the sharp bend of the Schoharie River about a half mile east of the eastern base of the Nose. Reciting: "I promised the several sachems when I bought the land of them that Ca-rae-ahdun-kah [Indian chief] should be allowed to live where he now lives so long as he chooses, and reserve for his use [the land] where he lives."

Most of the prehistoric occupancy of the Schoharie Valley seems to be related to an influx from the Hudson Valley (which parallels the Schoharie about twenty miles to the east) and to the early occupants of the lower Mohawk River to the northeast. The latter people probably moved into the Schoharie Valley by crossing the Helderbergs or by following the ancient glacial valley separating the Mariaville and Rotterdam hills from the Helderhills.

To my knowledge the only site with roots to the west in the Susquehanna watershed was found about 50 years ago near Gilboa, when high water eroded some of the property of Fred Stryker. The flooding uncovered a small prehistoric site that disclosed decorated potsherds similar to those found at the Castle Creek site along the Chenango —

a major tributary of the Susquehanna River near
Bainbridge, New York.

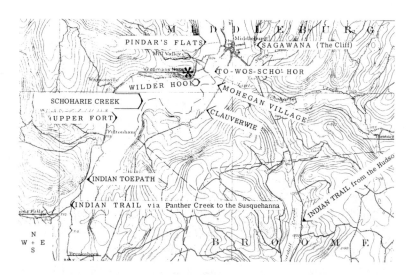

Location of important areas around Vroomans Nose (*).

Settlement of Vroomansland

CONFLICT OVER THE LAND and personal safety started with the first attempt by colonists to occupy the Schoharie Valley. The fertile flats bordering the Schoharie River held priority in the Dutch mind, so that in 1712 Adam Vrooman, a survivor of the Schenectady Massacre and a freeholder of that village, purchased from the Schoharie Indians the extensive flats west of the river and east and south of Vroomans Nose, known by the Indians as Mount Onistagrawa. This deed for about 600 acres of the Schoharie Flats and adjacent uplands, and which included Vroomans Nose, was signed by 18 members of the Turtle, Wolf, and Bear Clans. The Royal Patent for this land was executed on August 26, 1714. On March 30, 1726, an amended "Correction Deed," which covered all of Vroomansland — the flats extending southwesterly and southerly from Line Creek (the boundary between Middleburgh and Fulton townships) and the area east of what is now Watsonville and Fultonham — was obtained from Nahragoe (Bear), Kahahighead (Wolf) and Sudararykan (Turtle) and six other Indians. This added land totaled about 1,200 acres and is still some of the most fertile and productive land in the valley.

In 1714, Adam Vrooman built a stone house on the flats near the base of Vroomans Nose. Before it was occupied, a group of Palatines who had come from Livingston Manor and settled in the vicinity of Weiser's Dorf (Middleburgh) and who were led by Conrad Weiser, demolished the structure. The Palatines felt that this was land promised them by Queen Anne in 1709 before they migrated from England; however, they had never obtained a written land deed. Ill feelings continued between the Dutch, mainly the Vroomans of Schenectady, and the Palatines.

Adam Vrooman complained to Governor Hunter on July 9, 1715, that the Palatines from Weiser's Dorf had destroyed the stone house that he had nearly completed. A judgment from Governor Hunter favoring Vrooman was rendered, which effectively removed this legal problem. As a result, many of the Palatines left the area, migrating down the Susquehanna River to Tulpehocken, Berks County, Pennsylvania. Others moved north along the Mohawk River to Palatine Bridge and Stone Arabia. Some went to Canada. The fertile flats extending from Line Creek, which flowed along the north side of the Nose, to near the stream that enters the Schoharie at the present village of Fultonham, were soon divided into six farms occupied by the sons and a daughter of Adam Vrooman. Part of the land acquired by Adam Vrooman was Vroomans Nose. In the mid-1700s the uplands were owned by Vroomans named Daniel, Josias, Adam and Bartholomew. Adjacent to this land were lands owned by William Johnson, and the Byrne and Butler patents. This bottom land is some of the most fertile in the Northeast and has produced annual crops for more than 275 years.

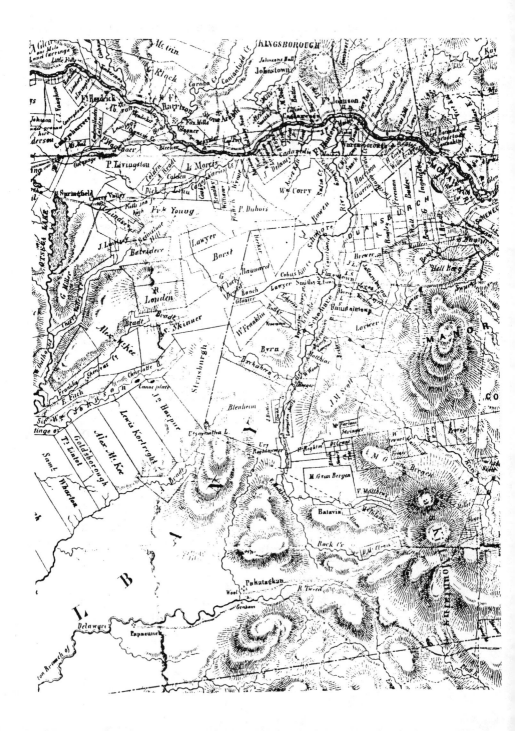

The Schenectady Connection

ADAM VROOMAN, who established Vroomansland, was born in Holland in 1649, the son of Hendrick Meese Vrooman. At the age of 21 he bound himself as an apprentice to Cornelius Van den Berg of Albany County to learn the millwright's trade. Thirteen years later he built a mill on the Sand Kill in Schenectady, where he lived and owned considerable property.

During the Schenectady Massacre in 1690, his wife and infant son were killed and two sons, Wouter and Barent, were carried away to Canada by the French and Indian invaders. In 1698, he went to Canada to obtain the release of his sons and two relatives. He died at Vroomansland, February 25, 1730, but was buried in Schenectady. Adam married three times and had thirteen children, all but two of them living at the time of his death. His mill on the Sand Kill and the land in its valley were transferred to his son, Wouter, in 1710.

Adam Vrooman owned considerable property in Schenectady and its environs including mills, a brew house, and farmlands, all of which he willed to his children. His major land holdings, however, were in the Schoharie

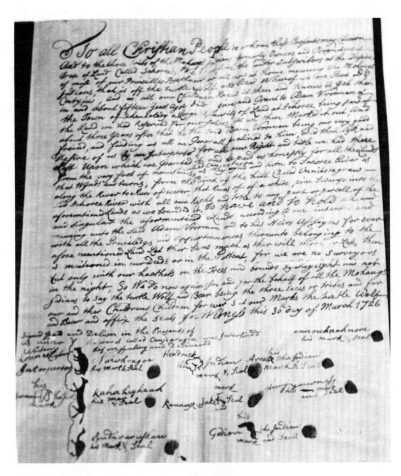

LEFT. Deed granted to Adam Vrooman in 1711 concerning the lands which later were called Vroomansland. Signed by three chiefs of the Mohawk representing the Turtle, Wolf, and Bear clans.

ABOVE. Another Mohawk deed granted to Adam Vrooman in 1726 which was meant to include the Schoharie flats extending from Middleburgh to the Watsonville area.

Valley. He was buried in a family plot at 35 Front Street within the Schenectady stockade but his remains were eventually removed, possibly to the Vrooman Cemetery located near the end of Filmore Street in Woodlawn, which is cared for by the Town of Niskayuna.

Vroomansland Massacre

DURING THE PREPARATION of this publication several persons have requested that the story of the Vroomansland massacre be added. An article was written in 1984 by Sylvia Van Houten for the Stone Fort Days booklet published by the Schoharie County Historical Society. We herein add the content of her article. The Van Houtens live under the brow of Vroomans Nose and daily raise their eyes to view the mountain with its rock ledges.

It's hard to imagine that a massacre occurred near the garden where today we peacefully hoe our corn. The mountain known as Vromans Nose looms 600 feet overhead to the north. Our sturdy Dutch barn shades from the south. Vromans Nose is also known as Onistagrawa, "corn mountain" in the Iroquois tongue, for near its base Indians tilled their corn (maize). It was here the Vroman's land massacre occurred.

The later years of the Revolution were bloody years for the Schoharie Valley. Although three protecting forts were in the valley, people were very unprotected when they left the forts to work in their homes, barns, and fields. The rich harvests, much of which were sent to Washington's army, thus earning the area in the title "Breadbasket of the Revolution," made the valley prey to a number of crop destroying raids.

August 9, 1780 marked the third raid of the summer, later to become known as the Vroman's land massacre. Scouts had sighted a war party of about 80 Indians and Tories, led by Joseph Brant, a Mohawk. One scout barely reached the Upper Fort in time to sound the cannon alarm before the invaders struck. Some who heard ran to hide.

Ephraim Vroman's family hid in their orchard and nearby cornfield. Mrs. Vroman, not seeing her husband for a moment, called out to him, consequently, alerting the enemy to their whereabouts. She and her four-year-old daughter were found and killed in the cornfield. When an Indian and Ephraim grappled for a spear, Ephraim's five-month-old infant thought it a game and giggled and laughed at the "sport." Evidently the laugh softened the aggressor, and instead of death, he made prisoners of father and child.

Tunis Vroman and his four sons had gone out to harvest wheat and his wife was doing the week's wash. She was struck down in her kitchen. Tunis and one son were shot or tomahawked near the wheat barrack. The other sons were captured.

Abraham Vroman was on his haywagon near the Swart home when the alarm sounded. He picked up Judge Swart, his wife, Cornelia and baby. They started off just as the enemy reached the Swart's place. Vroman and his strong team of horses did not stop to open the gate but crashed right through and made it safely to the fort.

Some made it safely to the fort as did Abraham Vroman and the Swarts, but many did not. Men, women and children were killed in their homes and fields. Houses, barns, and crops were torched, and livestock killed. The invaders moved on up the valley driving about 90 captured horses and about 30 prisoners.

The victims lay dead and scalped along the flats below the mountain. The next day they were buried in the Upper Fort Cemetery. On most of the stones was the name "Vroman."

In our garden we find bits and pieces of that other time. Musketballs, broken clay pipe bowls and stems, buttons, coins, pieces of dishes, and flint work their way to the surface. Now, as we hoe, a tractor motor sounds in the distance. The red tail hawks and turkey buzzards soar on the mountain's updrafts, and beaver in the Muddy Brook slap their tails in the water. Silently, Vromans Nose continues to overlook it all.

6—View from top of Onistagrawa Mountain, Middleburg, N. Y.

Post card view of Van Houten farm from Vroomans Nose.

Defense of Schoharie Valley

THE SETTLERS of Vroomansland enjoyed more than 50 years of relative peace after the initial problems with the Palatines, many of whom had left by 1729. Then with the developing threat of the American Revolution, the valley dwellers decided in the spring of 1777 to erect three bastions. The southernmost or Upper Fort was located southeast of Vroomans Nose south of the site of the Indian settlement cited in the original deed received by Adam Vrooman which excepted the Indian village. An Indian castle was originally established by Sir William Johnson at the settlement located close to a backwater of the Schoharie River. The Upper Fort was located on property owned by John Feeck near today's Fultonham, midway across the wide upper flats where a rectangular area of about two and a half acres was staked out to include the Feeck buildings. Today the old Feeck burial plot is all that remains.

The Middle Fort was located east of the Schoharie River at the north entrance of the present village of Middleburgh, with the two story stone house of Johannes Becker as the center of the stockaded three acres. The

Lower Fort included an acre of land with its center the Dutch Reformed Church of Schoharie built in 1772 which is now the Schoharie County Museum, and the head-quarters of the Schoharie County Historical Society. It is located on the north end of the village of Schoharie near Foxes Creek.

Upper Fort at Fultonham

From the beginning of the Revolution, troubles beset the Schoharie Valley. The first problems involved a question of allegiance. There were some who opposed the war preferring to retain ties with the British Crown. These Tories were in the minority but owned some of the better valley farms. With the approach of the war, the fertile flats along the Schoharie assumed major importance when the wheat and corn grown there became the mainstay of provisions for Washington's army.

The occasional raids which marked the earlier part of the war mounted to a crescendo on October 17, 1780, when Sir John Johnson, son of Sir William, leading more than five hundred troops and Indian Captain Joseph Brant, leading several hundred Indian braves, entered the valley from the southwest by way of Panther Creek (today south of the entrance of Max V. Shaul State Park). The main objective of this raid was to destroy the grain which had recently been harvested. Saughtering all livestock in

Middle Fort at Weiserstown

their path, the invaders put the torch to the barns and other storage facilities as well as houses. It has been said that at least 100,000 bushels of wheat were destroyed during this raid.

The invaders tried to slip past the Upper Fort and strike a sudden, unexpected, fatal blow on the Middle Fort. However, the troops were not set into motion as early as intended. A farmer missed his stray cow, and when the troops were crossing the river near the Upper Fort, they were discovered and the alarm was sounded. They moved northward on the east side of the river, igniting all in their path, passed the Nose and attacked the Middle Fort. The battle raged for nearly eight hours. It was here that local hero Tim Murphy defied Major Woolsey, the Commandant of the Middle Fort, and fired three separate times upon British flag of truce. Woolsey surrendered his command to Colonel Peter Vrooman. The battle continued. Finally, convinced that the fort could not be conquered,

Lower Fort at Fox's Dorf

and after destroying all unprotected structures and livestock, the invaders moved on down the valley toward the Lower Fort. Very few of the garrison were injured, although the enemy suffered much greater losses. At the Lower Fort, sharpshooters were stationed in the bell tower and the enemy tired. Although at least three cannon shots were fired at the Lower Fort no damage was done. Fortunately, the loss of life was very small; however, many homes and barns were leveled. The year's harvest was destroyed and the Schoharie Valley lay in ruin.

Traveling over an ancient Indian path, the enemy continued northward toward the Mohawk, camping overnight

at the big bend of the Schoharie just south of Sloansville.
The route traveled went by the edge of the Great Stone
Heap, a short distance north of Sloansville where a huge
pile of stones had developed when each Indian who passed
it contributed a stone. (This stone heap was said to be
more than sixty feet long, twenty feet wide and five to

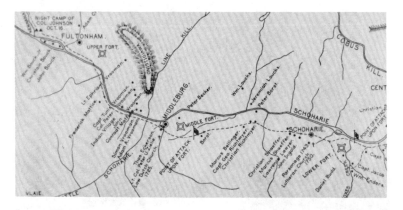

Route of Joseph Brant's raid. October 17, 1780.

fifteen feet high. Although greatly diminished in height,
this ancient relic is still to be seen in a grove of trees west
of Route 162 as it ascends toward the highlands of Charleston.) The route followed by Sir John and his troops can
still be seen in places as it follows the height of the land
existing between the precipitous streams running down
toward the Schoharie River to the east and Auries Creek
to the west. Reaching the Mohawk Valley, most of Sir
John's Iroquois friends headed west while his Regulars
and Tory allies forded the river just above the Schoharie's
confluence with the Mohawk west of Fort Hunter.

Footprints in the Valley

"I see them, the footprints of Timothy Murphy! They are still there. Look closely! You can still see them.

"Follow the light green field near the small stream just below the mountain edge. They are darker green than the rest."

This, from a French foreign exchange student, who had caught the spirit of the legend as we stood overlooking the verdant farmland between the Nose and the Schoharie River. We were standing on the very edge from which Tim made his famous jump to escape his pursuers. This is but one of the tales told about our folk hero.

One day Tim's cow had gone dry and he had to go to a neighbor's in the nearby hollow for milk. On his return home he carried a full pail in each hand. There was no way to carry his faithful double-barreled flintlock rifle. He was spotted by two Indians. Feeling this was their opportunity to end the career of the famous marksman and Indian fighter they gave chase. He outran them but came to the summit edge of the cliff. There was but one escape: to jump.

He landed safely. His pursuers no longer followed him. No milk had been spilled. (Some add to the story and say that it had all turned to butter on the way down.) However, he had a problem. He was stuck in the shale and mud up to his knees and couldn't pull his boots out. What a dilemma! What could he do? You guessed it. He ran home. Got a shovel, returned and dug himself out.

The stories are many, and Tim is the most colorful hero of the Schoharie Valley. He did exist and was well known for his agility of mind and body and expert marksmanship. He served as a scout for Washington's commissioned Morgan's Rifle Corps. A monument on the Saratoga Battlefield credits him with the shot that killed General Fraser, resulting in Burgoyne's defeat, a defeat which turned the tide of the Revolution in favor of the Americans.

Tim's brave, but insubordinate act, in defiance of Major Woolsey at the Middle Fort during the Johnson-Brant Raid, saved the day. He fought in nearly every well-known battle from Bunker Hill to Yorktown. Returning to the Schoharie Valley after the Revolution, he built a home and farmed near the Upper Fort across from the present home of Roger and Grace Barber. He also was a not-too-profitable real estate agent, buying and selling lands for others in the area. His contributions to local politics and the community were many.

Tim Murphy was born in 1751 in Minisink, New Jersey. His marriage to his beloved Margaret Feeck, with whom he had eloped, resulted in the birth of eight children. After her death he moved to South Worcester and married Mary Robertson, who bore him five children. He returned to the Schoharie Valley near the brow of Vroomans Nose. He died of pneumonia at his home in Fultonham in 1818 after trying to rescue his friend Judge John Brown and his two sons from the cold, turbulent Schoharie River during a spring freshet. Many of his descendants are living today in the area. His powderhorn, Bible, watch, snowshoe and will are at the Old Stone Fort Museum. His will testifies to the fact that he never learned to read or write. It carries only the initials "TM," and was witnessed by his neighbor, William C. Bouck, a young lawyer, who was to become New York State's 13th governor in 1843.

Upon his death he was buried by the side of Margaret in the old Feeck Cemetery near his home. In 1872 his body and supposedly that of his first wife were moved to the "new" Middleburgh Cemetery, overlooking the flats and with Vrooman's Nose the center of vision.

On October 17, 1910, 130 years after the Johnson-Brant Raid his descendants, the Fosters and the community erected an eight foot granite slab with a bronze relief of a scout attired in buckskins resting the butt of a musket on the ground. Evelyn Longman was the sculptor. The inscription reads:

TO THE MEMORY OF
1751 TIMOTHY MURPHY 1818
PATRIOT, SOLDIER, SCOUT, CITIZEN,
WHO SERVED IN MORGAN'S RIFLE CORPS,
FOUGHT AT SARATOGA AND MONMOUTH
AND WHOSE BRAVERY REPELLED THE ATTACK
OF BRITISH AND THEIR INDIAN ALLIES
UPON THE MIDDLE FORT, OCTOBER 17, 1780,
AND SAVED THE COLONISTS OF
THE SCHOHARIE VALLEY

Yes, if you stand on the summit ledge of Vroomans Nose, overlooking the Valley toward the east, and look carefully, you too, can see his footprints.

The restored appearance of the residence of TIMOTHY MURPHY the noted HERO who held the Middle Fort contrary to the positive orders of his Commander. Oct. 17. 1780.

LEFT ABOVE. Home of Tim Murphy. Detail: the Girder Drawing.
LEFT BELOW. Early signatures including Tim Murphy's.
Both in Old Stone Fort Museum, Schoharie.
ABOVE. Marker and grave of Tim Murphy, Middleburgh Cemetery.
Vroomans Nose is in the background.

As a Movie Set

DURING THE 1930s a movie was produced using the south-facing cliff of the Nose on its western end. At that time the General Electric Company had a moving picture division as part of its publicity department. As an advertising gimmick for pushing a line of household appliances, GE developed a theme of "Pathfinders." The pathfinder selected was Timothy Murphy and the actor representing him was *me*.

The script had me dressed in a leather-fringed jacket, breeches and a coonskin cap and I carried a flintlock musket. As part of the pathfinding action I had to wade the Sacandaga River with an ice-fringed shore, emerge from a dense woods in the Helderbergs and finally climb the cliff at Vroomans Nose.

The "rushes" were satisfactory and the job was done. After watching the film several times to catch any inconsistencies I suddenly saw something which was out of order. On the very last shot as my leather boot was moving upward, I was horrified to see the rubber heel of my hiking boot! I can still see it! Needless to say, the last part of that final shot soon lay on the cutting room floor!

Soldier, Defender, and Delegate

At THE OLD STONE FORT in Scho-
harie stands a monument erected October 17, 1913 to the
memory of Colonel Peter B. Vrooman, outstanding
patriot, soldier, representative of the Schoharie Valley
and well-known merchant. He was born at Vrooman's
Island, the son of Barent A. Vrooman and Engelite Swart,
June 20, 1735; died at Schoharie, N.Y., December 29,
1793. The original red sandstone marker, denoting his
final resting place, stands on a knoll overlooking his home
and the site of his mill on Fox's Creek. It was here that he
moved soon after the Revolution, his buildings under
Vroomans Nose having been burned by an early raid on
the valley. Today, his beautiful colonial home is owned by
Mildred Vrooman, a direct descendant.

Peter Barent Vrooman was commissioned lieutenant
in 1754, captain in 1759, major in 1770, under the Crown,
and served against the French on the frontier. Upon the
declaration of war he espoused the cause of the Colonies,
and was commissioned colonel of 15th Regiment, Albany

County Militia by the Provincial Congress of New York on October 20, 1775. He dropped the "B" in his name, perhaps to shield himself from being recognized as the former major of the British government. He remained in command from the beginning to the close of the Revolution, excepting when reinforcements were sent to the valley or when by reason of courtesy or seniority of rank, was transferred to the visiting commandment. During Johnson's invasion, Colonel Peter Vrooman was the superior officer and took part in the defense of the Middle Fort. The Continental major was either a coward or traitor, as he insisted on giving admittance to the flag of truce, upon which Colonel Vrooman took command, even issuing the ammunition himself, that the men might not know the scantiness of the supply, and thus by his boldness and determination, and with the help of the other defenders of the valley, saved the fort.

In addition to his military service, Colonel Vrooman held the office of secretary to the Committee of Safety, was elected to Continental Congress in 1775, was member of Assembly in 1777, 1779 and 1786, and served as delegate to the General Committee. Elected a delegate to the New York State Convention which ratified the United States Constitution July 26, 1788 at Poughkeepsie, New York, he was a friend and associate of Anti-Federalists John Lansing, Jr., Governor George Clinton, and Robert Yates. He returned to his home in Schoharie just before the vote was taken. However, his attendance is recorded in the life-sized mural by Gerald Foster which is on the wall of the Poughkeepsie post office showing the closing moments of New York State's ratification of the Constitution.

Col. Peter Vrooman (seated). Mural in Poughkeepsie post office.

The Common Lands

THE SOUTHERN BOUNDARY lands of Vroomans Nose consist of great talus slopes which have been accumulating since the glacier melted some 10,000 years ago. Their southernmost edge is skirted by NYS Route 30 which extends from the Village of Trout at the New York-Quebec border in the northern Adirondacks to the southwestern Catskill Mountains where it ends near the Pennsylvania border at NYS Route 17. The northernmost portion of the talus slope of Vroomans Nose ends at the cliff face where the Hamilton sandstones and shales are exposed. This is the area termed the Common Lands and have been so shown on early maps of the region.

Such lands are the property of the people of the Township of Fulton. Until Fulton was formed in 1828 it was part of the Town of Middleburgh. In colonial days the common lands could be employed as a source of firewood, grazing and other suitable uses. Such lands could be rented upon petition by an individual and approved by the town board after a public hearing. In certain cases that I am aware of, the lands could actually be sold to an individual following official action of a town board.

The southeastern end of the common lands of Vroomans Nose has been used for some years as a source of shale by the Town of Fulton and a private individual. This has produced an unsightly scar when viewed from the east. Efforts have been made to stop such activity since it could destabilize the cliff above. It is hoped that if future efforts are successful, suitable planting of shrubs and plants can be made to eventually heal the scar.

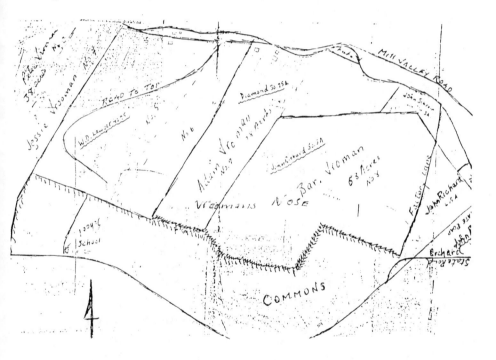

Land map showing property owned by the Vroomans in the 1800s.

Views

THE NOSE is a dramatic centerpiece of the natural features of the Schoharie Valley. While many other beauty spots and areas of great natural and historic interest are within the environs of the valley, Vroomans Nose has more diverse features than any of the others. From Fultonham it appears to block the valley, and from the first hill on the Clauverwie Road south out of Middleburgh following the east bank of the Schoharie River the widest profile of the Nose is visible. Its southern cliff face is quite spectacular. From Middleburgh and the summit of the cliff, it dominates the western view beyond the village, and from the north going south from Schoharie on NYS Route 30 it looms higher and higher as Middleburgh is approached along Route 30. The view of the Nose from NYS Route 145, the Livingstonville Road, south out of Middleburgh, shows the steep vertical cliff of its southeastern end in profile. This is best seen across the flood plain of the Little Schoharie just before the road leaves the plain and starts climbing toward the upper watershed of the Catskills and about halfway up the hill opposite the Middleburgh Cemetery along the road to Huntersland.

We hope that the barrow pit scar on the east end of the Commons which extends from Route 30 to the vertical cliff of the Nose can be erased by nature with some judicious assistance from man. From Route 30 as it skirts the base of the Nose along the Commons, it is almost impossible to see the Nose because of its very steep talus slope and vertical cliff face. This talus and cliff area is a virtual wilderness. The steepness of the talus and rather friable nature of the Hamilton beds discourage hiker and rock climber alike so that nature has been undisturbed in that region for millennia. The eastern and northern boundaries of the Nose are mostly wooded and are not unlike many other hillside areas of the valley. Only the lower slopes can seen from the road which follows the course of Line Creek. This secondary road leads into Mill Valley and West Middleburgh ("Polly Hollow") where some years ago there was a settlement inhabited by what were locally called the "Polly Hollow Sloughters."

Aerial Veiws
Above: View of northeast slope. BELOW: View of rock ledge and
dance floor, Route 30 at bottom. Photos by Harold Zoch.

View from Old Route 30. Hubbard home in foreground.

View from Saddlemore Hill, Clauverwie.

ABOVE.
View from Little Schoharie Creek at Hedgerow, Clauverwie.
Cattle of Larry Van Aller are in the foreground.

BELOW.
"Sky Island of the Schoharie Valley"
Early morning fog, July 1992.

Vromans Nose from the Cliff Middleburgh, N. Y.

Vroomans Nose on post cards.

ABOVE. From the Cliff, Middlebrugh.
BELOW. The Middleburgh covered bridge (second) across
Schoharie Creek. Completed in 1859, it was 300 feet long
and was replaced by an iron bridge in 1905.
Courtesy of Arthur U. Stevenson and John L. Warner.

Onistagrawa Mountain (Vroman's Nose), Middleburg, N. Y., Schoharie Co.

Vroomans Nose on post cards.

Aerial veiws.
ABOVE. South side.
BELOW. East side.
Photos by Harold Zoch.

From "Blue Hole," Schoharie Creek.

From Hardscrabble Road.

Farm Crops of Vroomansland

THE RICH BOTTOM LANDS of the Schoharie River flood plain have produced bounteous crops for more than two centuries. Originally, when this area was settled by Adam Vrooman, probably a wide diversity of crops was produced. It is likely that the original prehistoric and historic Indian settlers grew corn, squash and other foods before the colonists arrived, for the mountain's original name, means "Corn Mountain."

Later in the 1700s wheat became an important crop, and although peas and corn were grown, the Schoharie Valley became one of the largest "Bread Baskets of the Revolution." North of Schoharie the valley narrowed, the flats were much smaller, and less grain could be produced.

After the Revolution, the colonists rebuilt their churches, homes and barns and continued to till the rich lands, raising a variety of crops. There was one period during the last half of the nineteenth century when the flats north of Vroomansland were devoted entirely to the raising of hops. Two of the large barns used for drying the hops are

Agriculture.
ABOVE. From Route 145. Corn and alfalfa fields belonging to the
Beckers and Pindars. BELOW. From Huntersland Road.

Agriculture.
ABOVE. Hop growing in view of the Nose.
BELOW. Farm fields today.

still standing (1985). This lucrative crop was abandoned between the two world wars when blue mold could not be controlled, and the chemical manufacture of beer increased. The Midwest became the great hops producer, and at the present time, extensive hop farms have been developed along the Columbia and Yakima Rivers in eastern part of Washington State.

Until recently the major crops grown in the valley have been corn and alfalfa, used mainly as fodder for dairy cattle. Apple orchards have long been present, having been instituted by the first settlers. Today, however, a much wider variety of produce has taken over ranging from carrots to strawberries, raspberries, melons, squash, sweet corn, pumpkins, squash, potatoes, cabbage, peppers, tomatoes, peas, cauliflower, onions, broccoli and asparagus. The local farmer sells directly from his roadside farmstand to the consumer.

Early Settlement

As IN MANY EARLY COMMUNITIES that developed during the colonial period of 1711-1775, there were in the Schoharie Hills small settlements often comprised of a single extended family. It was essential that such enclaves become as self sufficient as possible.

Except for the rich flood plain soil of the main valley extending from Esperance to North Blenheim, the hills and lesser stream valley soils were relatively thin; but where there was weathered limestone, they produced good crops. The terrain favored the development of small communities which in turn led to considerable parochialism. Local names such as "The Sloughters" and "The Honeys" identified the inhabitants, not always in complimentary terms.

The settlement of Vroomansland, Watsonville, Mill Valley, Petersburgh, Pleasant Valley and Fultonham are typical of these developments. The valley of Line Creek was typical of such small settlements.

In the early years, hill roads left the main road which followed and climbed Line Creek westerly into the highlands. One of the most interesting of these roads has been

From *Beers Atlas*, 1866.

abandoned but still leads to the extensive cemetery of Patria where many early settlers are buried. Neglected for some years it has recently been cleared and put into commendable condition. Many of the abandoned farmlands of the Patria region were reforested by the Civilian Conservation Corps during the 1930s when the state obtained the title to many deserted, rundown farms. They are now a productive forest. By traveling over the West Middleburgh hill there was a direct route to Mineral Springs. This public highway has been closed for many years.

Role in World War II

SHORTLY AFTER THE START of World War II, Dr. Irving Langmuir, the first industrial scientist to receive the Nobel Prize, was a member of a governmental advisory board. I worked for him as his laboratory assistant. One day he came to me and sought my help in devising a method to make large quantities of smoke with the hope of using it to screen cities, beach-heads, ships, bridges and the like from air surveillance and bombing. (This was before the development of radar which would penetrate a smoke screen.)

Within a few weeks I had developed a smoke generator which gave promise of solving the problem. It was tested, first on top of the laboratory, then at the edge of the General Electric Works at Schenectady, then in the Cushing Gravel Pit along the Mohawk River. At each location the generator produced so much smoke that it was not possible to obtain any quantitative information about screening potential.

With this in mind, I suggested to Dr. Langmuir that it should be possible to obtain the measurements we needed by producing a smoke cloud on the flats of the Schoharie

ABOVE. Artificial fog generated with the Schaefer-Langmuir smoke generator. Photo from on the summit of Vroomans Nose by the author.

BELOW. Artificial fog being generated by an enlarged version of the Schaefer-Langmuir smoke generator. The ridge leading to Vroomans Nose is in the background. The final model of the generator was less than a fifth the size of this prototype. Photo by the author.

Valley while observing it from the top of Vroomans Nose. I took him out there, and he was immediately in agreement that it was a perfect spot. It was particularly timely since our preliminary tests were so promising that we were planning to use a generator which would make ten times as much smoke.

Initial tests were made on the Jenks Farm (now the home of Wallace Van Houten) just below the Nose, but the smoke was so widespread that we were forced to move further south and to choose the apple orchard of James G. Youmans (near the present home of Philip Bohringer). The tests made May 7 and May 12, 1942, were so impressive that plans were made to test the large generator using the central portion of Vroomansland on the farm of George C. Wilber. Preliminary tests were conducted on June 21 and 23, preparatory to a demonstration run on June 24, 1942, before an official group including seven representatives from the U.S. Army, eight from the Navy, an officer from the Canadian Army, nine representatives of the National Defense Research Committee, two from industrial concerns, five from the General Electric Research Laboratory, and one from Bloomfield, New Jersey.

On June 24, a caravan of cars and military vehicles left Schenectady about 4 a.m. and proceeded to the wood road along Line Creek. There we parked the cars and with military vehicles and on foot climbed the Nose. We had previously obtained permission from William D. Lawyer to use this road. We reached the summit of the Nose and were soon in radio communication with the crew at the generator site on the Wilber Farm. The dawn was cloudless and the air calm.

As soon as the flats of Vroomansland were visible we gave the order to start the generator which had the code name "Junior." It was a huge, bulky affair mounted on a heavy truck with a smokestack — a device which had been constructed by engineers of the Esso Research Laboratory in New Jersey in less than a month using discarded parts of old equipment.

Shortly after the order was given to start the generator, a white cloud could be seen forming and spreading out horizontally from the generator site. It was soon evident that strong uniform ground inversion which had a slight drift toward the north was present across the flats of Vroomansland. Within ten minutes a spectacular screening fog had formed which continued to spread toward the base of Vroomans Nose, hiding the apple orchards, barns, house and everything else across the flats. It continued to spread in a northerly direction, eventually passing east of the Nose and out of sight.

At the same time that the larger cloud was forming, our smaller General Electric generator located on the Jenks farm was started. Alongside it was another generator which had been officially approved by the Army's Chemical Warfare Division. It was a modified orchard heater that produced a thin black smoke. Both generators were using the same amount of fuel.

The comparison of the appearance and amount of smoke produced by these generators indicated clearly that the "official" generator was a very poor performer. We later learned that on the basis of this sorry performance a twenty-five million dollar order was canceled!

During the midst of cloud production by "Junior," Dr. Vladimir Zworykin, chief of research for the Radio Corporation of America, examined the terrain hidden by the smoke with his newly invented infrared telescope. He became quite excited when he observed that he could easily see through the smoke screen that hid all objects as seen in the visible range. I had previously found that I could do the same with infrared photography. However, his device could be used in real time.

Our visitors remained on top of Vroomans Nose until about 10:30 in the morning. They were quite elated with the evidence presented. Subsequently, we learned that more than fifty thousand of the big generators were ordered, built and used during the remainder of the war. They were used at the Anzio Beachhead in Italy, in North Africa, in the Rhine Crossings and for protecting ships from kamikaze attacks in the South Pacific.

An amusing sidelight occurred during the morning after our demonstration. Walking down the road that was being used by the jeeps for transporting some of our visitors, I took a picture of a jeep climbing the road to get another load. The picture later developed is one of the most dramatic I have ever photographed. However, I was warned not to use it or even to show it since the jeep at that time was a highly classified military secret!

Reaching the bottom of the Nose everyone was taken to the Wilbur generator site where "Junior" was located. It was operated so that the committee and other visitors could see the smoke production. It was an impressive sight to see the sonic velocity jets spewing out ten streams of vapor which quickly condensed to form the tiny spherical oil droplets which comprised the artificial fog. The droplets, being less than one 1/25,000 of an inch (0.6 uM — twenty times smaller than an ordinary fog droplet), had virtually no falling velocity so that they acted more like a gas than a particle and thus went wherever the air carried them. In addition to having very high persistence in the air, the fog particles were of the optimum size to scatter visible light most efficiently. It was an elegant solution to the screening problem.

Following the inspection of the generator, the entire group went to a restaurant in Middleburgh for lunch. While drinking a cup of coffee, thirty-six sleepless hours caught up with me and I dozed off. The splash of coffee awakened me and I managed to stay awake until I reached home.

Photo from Vroomans Nose by the author.

Land Ownership

WHEN ADAM VROOMAN originally acquired the lands in the Schoharie Valley, the uplands included all of the present lands of Vroomans Nose. On June 14, 1803, it was divided into eight parcels owned respectively (from the west) by Samuel, Josia C., Peter C., Josias C., Cornelius B., John B., Adam and Bartholomew Vrooman. At some later date these lands were all sold outside the Vrooman family. By the early 1900s, the upland slopes of the Nose were owned by W. D. Lawyer, John Rickard and John Diamond. In the 1930s the Nose was acquired by Arlington Van Dyke and his brother Arden. It was from the former and the estate of the latter that it was purchased in 1983 by the Vromans Nose Preservation Corporation.

It is likely that originally the uplands were used for a timber source and for the grazing of cattle. They were too precipitous and have such thin soil that tillage for crops was not feasible with the possible exception of hay on the lower northern and northeastern slopes.

In addition to very large hemlock and white pine trees, it is likely that the main crop of the forested slopes was

firewood of oak and hickory which grew on the terraces
that exist on the north side of the Nose. The wood road
which ascended the Nose from the north was probably
constructed for lumbering purposes. It is too steep for
pleasure cars but can be navigated by jeep and other
four-wheel-drive vehicles.

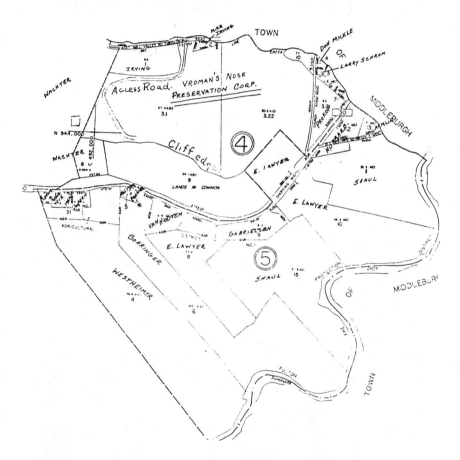

Tax map of the land owned by the
Vromans Nose Preservation Corporation.

The Long Path of New York

VROOMANS NOSE was the primary objective of the Long Path of New York as it entered the Schoharie Valley and moved north from the George Washington Bridge in New York City to Whiteface Mountain in the Adirondacks.

Originally, in 1931, I conceived of the Long Path as an outlet of the Appalachian Trail which would give a hiker the alternative of heading north for the Adirondacks rather than northeast into the Berkshires and eventually to Mt. Katahdin in Maine. Thus, my earliest route started at Bear Mountain and from there headed into the western slopes of the Catskills by way of Slide Mountain. After discussing the route with hikers from the New York-New Jersey area, we decided to originate the Path at the western end of the George Washington Bridge, then follow the eastern edge of the Palisades northward and from there head through the Ramapos across the Shawangunks and then toward and over Slide Mountain in the western Catskills. The route would then go into the upper drainage of the Schoharie and then into the middle Schoharie by way of Gilboa, Breakabeen and Middleburgh.

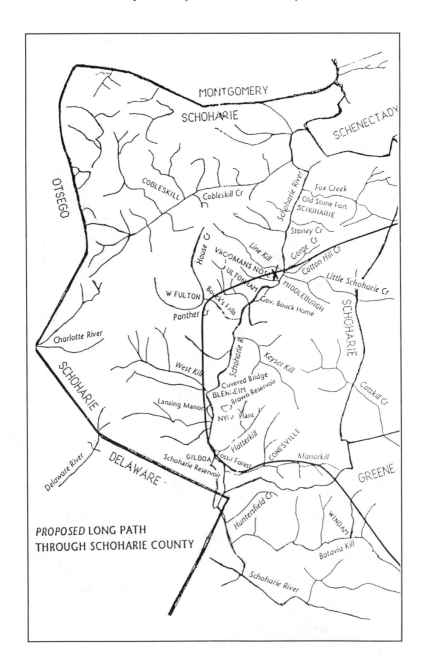

PROPOSED LONG PATH
THROUGH SCHOHARIE COUNTY

Following the eastern side of the valley north of Gilboa, it would then cross the river near Breakabeen up Panther Creek to Boucks Falls and thence into the high country southwest of Vroomans Nose. From there it would move easterly to the ridge that climbs to the cap rock of the Nose.

The Long Path then would descend the jeep road to Line Creek into Mill Valley or as an alternative go down the steep eastern slope of the Nose at the Middleburgh end. Continuing easterly, the Long Path would cross the Schoharie at the Middleburgh bridge, head easterly to the trail which climbs to the top of the "Cliff" above Middleburgh and then would go northeasterly over Dutch Billy's Hill to the Helderberg Plateau. It would go to Indian Ladder to the northern end of the escarpment where it would descend to Altamont, and head northwestward up the Bozenkill to the Christman Wildlife Sanctuary, now protected by the Nature Conservancy. The Adirondack-type lean-to at the Upper Falls on the Bozenkill was originally built by the Mohawk Valley Hiking Club to serve as an overnight shelter for Long Path hikers.

I should point out that the Long Path as originally planned followed the basic theme of Walt Whitman, who said, "There lies before me a long brown path leading wherever I choose." I planned the Path as a route which would be marked on the USGS topographic maps and which would employ secondary roads, abandoned roads, wood paths and trails wherever possible. Where they didn't exist the traveler would bushwhack using the map and a compass to move in the general direction shown on the map. Thus it was an original "orienteering" procedure, a type of outdoor game that has become quite popular here in the Northeast.

The other basic purpose of the Path was to unite many of the unique beauty spots and areas of geological, prehistoric, historic or natural science importance. Thus Vrooman's Nose was a perfect example of the objective since it combined all of these features.*

There is an increasing trend in the use of the restored Long Path. An effort will be made to have information on it available at the Old Stone Fort in Schoharie, headquarters of the Schoharie County Historical Society, and with the Vromans Nose Preservation Corporation.

* Since Dr. Schaefer's conception of the Long Path in 1931 (described in the **New York Post** on March 29, 1934) various other routes have been discussed. However, all seemed to fade until 1960 when the New York-New Jersey Trail Conference revived the project. Since then, volunteers have constructed and are maintaining the first 225 miles of trail from New Jersey to the northern Catskills. In 1976 the trail was completed to Windham in Greene County. Its direction to the Mohawk River remained to be designated.

During 1991 Dale Hughes of the Trail Conference and Eric Hollman, the River and Trail Planner for the Conservation Assistance Program of the National Parks Service, through their visual presentations to many organizations, and in consultation with Dr. Schaefer, renewed public interest and the determination to finalize the designation of the last 75 miles. Schoharie County was the last link.

The first section, from Windham to Durham and then along the Schoharie-Greene border by the Schoharie Reservoir and Minekill State Park through the Schoharie Valley and through state forest lands in Blenheim, was easily determined. From there three routes were proposed:

1.) Western: pass through state lands in Summit and Richmondville, veer into Otsego County and onto state land in Decator, Rosebloom and Cherry Valley, enter Montgomery County, and reach the Mohawk through Springfield, Stark and Minden.

2.) Central: Turn east through the Town of Fulton, swing north into Middleburgh, Schoharie and Esperance, cross state lands in Charleston, Montgomery County, pass through Glen and end in Auriesville on the Mohawk.

3.) Eastern: Cross the woodlands of Fulton, pass over Vromans Nose, cross the Schoharie River at Middleburgh, pass through Middleburgh's Main Street, pass through The Gorge, cut northeast over Cotton Hill, enter state land in Berne, Albany County, and follow the Helderberg Ridge through Schenectady County to the Mohawk.

About 70 people from 27 organizations and agencies participated in the meetings, mapping, field trips, and evaluations. At the October meeting of the New York-New Jersy Trail Conference the decision was announced by Howard Dash, Long Path Chairman: "We felt Plattekill Park, the Helderbergs and Vromans Nose were outstanding resources and the overall scenic value of the eastern route was the highest of the three." Thus, Dr. Schaefer's original route was selected and will become reality. The goal for completion is 1996. —Helene S. Farrell, 1992

Climbing the Nose

THERE ARE THREE ROUTES to reach the summit of Vroomans Nose. One is an easy ascent. The other two are steep and difficult.

The easiest approach is from the official parking lot on the north side. The parking lot was improved through the efforts of the Middleburgh Lions Club. This route follows an old wood road that in dry weather can be negotiated with a jeep or other four-wheel drive vehicle. Unless the individual is handicapped, I'd strongly recommend walking, since the old road is an easy climb and passes beautiful trees and wildflowers (see the next chapter for detailed hiking directions).

This road ascends a number of wooded terraces. It passes some very large white pine and hemlock trees on the right with smaller evergreens covering the steep slope on the left. A number of flat terraces are encountered on the left (east), which if followed, open up occasionally into small meadows. Deer trails cross these terraces in several places.

After climbing about a half mile, the wood road reaches the col which separates the ridge that descends from Patria and the final summit of Vrooman's Nose, which rises about 75 feet in an easterly direction. This is the end of the wood road. A rocky trail continues to the top. This climbs over several protruding ledges of the Hamilton shales and sandstones comprising the Nose.

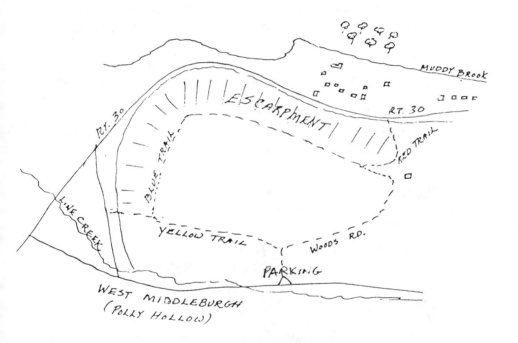

The summit consists of a flat layer of hard sandstone profusely scratched by the glacier. Except for the "Dance Floor" an area at the western end of the Nose which has been stripped of the soil covering the top of the Nose, a thin layer of sandy soil supports dense patches of huckleberry, bearberry and grass with a scattering of brush and small trees (red cedar, chestnut oak, and hickories).

A bushwhacking trail goes up the extreme eastern slope of the Nose. It has little to recommend it as a route for reaching the summit. When used, it provides a fast though precipitous descent to the valley, but is not recommended.

A third trail of sorts climbs the southwestern side. It ascends the talus slope, and while not as steep as the eastern route, it also is not recommended, except as a quick route down the summit where it intersects NYS Route 30.

The wood road ascending the northerly slope is by far the nicest route to the summit.

Early hikers. Collection of Helene S. Farrell.

Hiking Directions

SEE MAP for **woods road, red, blue,** and **yellow** trails:

1. **Easiest trail** — From traffic light at intersection of Route 30 and Route 145 on west end of Middleburgh bridge, go .6 mile south, turn right at old gas station on West Middleburgh, go .7 mile, about 100 yards beyond small bridge across Line Creek. Park car at parking lot (note parking on map), walk across field and find woods road, follow it up until top of cliff (about .6 mile). Top of cliff trail is about .3 mile long. On the eastern end, a view of village of Middleburgh is possible.

2. **Steepest and shortest trail** — This trail has **red** paint markers on trees it is located on the southern slope of Vroomans Nose about 1.6 miles south on Rt. 30 from traffic light. The beginning of the trail is located close to P. Bohringer's mailbox about 100 yards east of tavern on Rt. 30. Follow red markers up hill: the trail will reach the western edge of Vroomans Nose property. At top turn right and follow ridge to top of cliff trail.

3. **Medium steep trail** — This trail has blue markers on trees. It is located about .9 mile south on Rt. 30 from traffic light. Turn right on dirt road at base of eastern wooded slope of Vroomans Nose (nearly opposite Old Rt. 30). Go about .2 mile down this road to about 100' before white church. Walk up old road to shale quarry, then go right following blue markers on trees.

A circle route is possible by starting at parking lot on West Middleburgh road (#1 trail) and picking up #3 trail (blue markers) at eastern end of top of cliff. When reaching intersection of **yellow** and **blue** trail, take **yellow** trail back to parking lot.

For information on hiking, contact Harold Vroman of Cobleskill or Wally Van Houten, who lives on Route 30 at the foot of the southern slope of Vroomans Nose (Vroomans Nose information sign is in front of the Van Houten house). Both are members of the Vromans Nose Preservatiuon Corporation.

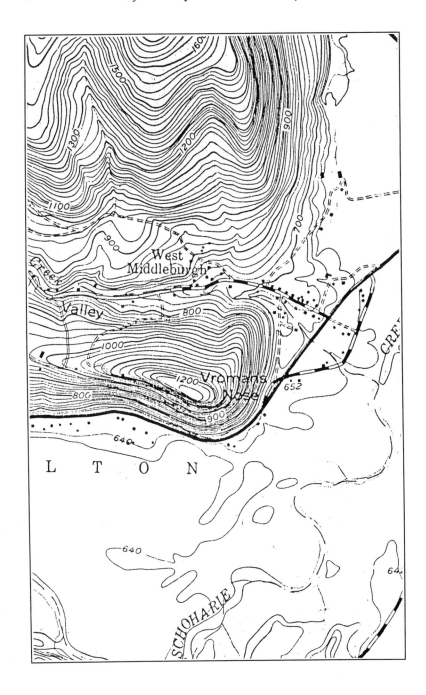

Protection for Posterity

MORE THAN 50 YEARS AGO, Judge F. Walter Bliss of Middleburgh made an effort to preserve Vroomans Nose by having it acquired and designated a New York State Park. With the help of William Ruland, he prepared a report along with photographs and a map, which on July 5, 1935, was submitted to the Schoharie County Planning Board. Earlier in 1935, a resolution was passed by the Schoharie County Conservation Association with copies sent to Assemblyman William S. Dunn, Senator Walter W. Stokes, Parks Commissioner Robert Moses and State Conservation Commissioner Lithgow Osborne in the effort to secure legislation for the acquisition of the Nose so that it could become public land. Apparently this effort came to naught, for nothing tangible developed from this political effort.

At about the same time, I, independently, became impressed with the unique features of the Nose and began to wonder if there were some way to protect it from possible abuses in the future. This interest was sharpened following our experiences in World War II and an increasing interest in the Schoharie Valley. Apparently others, including the

Schoharie County Historical Society, residents of the neighboring area, and members of the Vrooman descendants had the same concern.

By the 1970s I was somewhat discouraged at the possibility of establishing the Nose as an historical landmark when I learned that the current owner was talking about building a restaurant on the summit, even though the logistics such as access, water, sewerage, etc. seemed insurmountable. The construction of a home and barns a short distance west of the summit rock ocurred at about the same time so that I decided to see what might be done.

I was able to interest Dr. George Cooley of the Nature Conservancy and guided him in company with Dr. Victor Cahalane to the summit. I was pleased to note their high enthusiasm. Subsequently, at Dr. Cooley's invitation, a regional director of the Conservancy accompanied us to the summit of the Nose. While he seemed interested from a personal standpoint, he pointed out that recently adopted criteria for site acquisition promulgated by the national board were such that the Nose property could not qualify.

Meanwhile, George and I learned that independently, several lineal descendants of Adam Vrooman, who were members of the Schoharie County Historical Society, had become very interested in the acquisition and preservation of the Nose. However, they alone were unable to meet the selling price but they were prepared to provide a conciderable sum of money toward its acquisition. At the same time, the Schoharie County Historical Society through Director Helene Farrell, President Rudolph Snyder and Trustees Harold Vroman, Edward Hagan and Harold Zoch indicated the society's interest in spearheading a drive to organize the purchase. The owner and estate contributed through the lowering of the original selling price. Mr. Vroman asked me to speak before the Cobleskill and Middleburgh Rotary Clubs to enlist their support for the project. I presented illustrated talks before the service clubs in the early spring of 1983. Mr. Vroman and the society continued to make presentations and many personal contacts. The public interest generated in this manner was sufficient to provide funds to match and surpass the $5,000 pledge that had been given toward the project by Dr. George Cooley.

[Dr. Schaefer and Dr. Cooley approached the Schoharie County Historical Society several times over the years with little or no response, although several members were extremely interested and concerned. The society, learning that the property was for sale, approached the State of New York Department of Parks and Recreation with maps and surveys and a field trip to the summit of the Nose. However, the state offered no support or encouragement and again all progress stagnated. It was reported to the society that Mr. Van Dyke would agree to a decrease in the sale price if the society was interested. In turn the society contacted Drs. Schaefer and Cooley, and a meeting was held with the society's executive board and Mrs. Williams of the Nature Conservancy. Dr. Cooley made an offer to contribute $5,000 if his pledge was matched. The society's board of directors contacted the interested Vrooman family members, its membership and the community. With the knowledge that one of the purposes of the Schoharie County Historical Society is, "to preserve historic sites. . .by acquisition if necessary," at the 1983 spring meeting of the society Mr. Wallace Van Houten made the motion that started the legal authorization so that the historical society could raise and collect the $42,000 for purchase to be held and channeled into a new corporation, when it could be formed. — Helene S. Farrell]

The property that had originally been divided among the children of Adam Vrooman was thus purchased through the Schoharie County Historical Society supported by large contributions of the lineal descendants of Adam Vrooman, (daughters of Robert and Geraldine Vroman: Terri V. Hartmann, Susan V. Walker, Margaret V. Nowak; and Harold B. Vroman) the membership of the society which included Drs. Schaefer and Cooley, and the community at large. A not-for-profit corporation, the Vromans Nose Preservation Corporation, was formed to take title to the property. Attorney Raynor Duncombe prepared the legal papers which were approved and signed by Secretary of State, The Hon. Gail Schaffer, a native of the upper valley (Blenheim). She participated in the dedication ceremonies held, November 3, 1984, at the Middleburgh Elementary School Lobby, whose windows afforded a full view of Vroomans Nose.

Appendix A

The Vromans Nose Preservation Corporation
Charter Officers and Directors

President: Teri V. Hartmann, Reistertown, Maryland
Vice-President: Harold B. Vroman, Cobleskill, New York
Secretary: Susan V. Walker, Sandwich, Massachusetts
Treasurer: Doris M. Vroman, Cobleskill, New York
Directors:
Margaret V. Nowak
Preston W. Hartmann
Robert Sherman
Rudolph D. Snyder
Helene S. Farrell
George Cooley, honorary member
Honorary Director: Dr. Vincent J. Schaefer
Executive Director: Harold B. Vroman
Administrator: Wallace Van Houten, Fultonham Road,
     Star Route, Middleburgh, New York

Appendix B

Ode to Vromans Nose
delivered at the dedication of the
Vromans Nose Preservation Corp.

"Let Us Look and Listen to The Mountain."
Today, for a short time all eyes are focused upon me.
I am Mt. Onistagrawa — Vroomans Nose.
My history lies in what you see, and what I have seen since
    the beginning.
Formed of sediments of a great lake, molded by the glacier
    whose ice flow left forever its marks upon my rocks, I
    sit in majestic silence to be seen by all who climb to my
    summit, pass near my brow, or look down from the
    heavens above.
I pass no judgments. Utter no sound.
My inspiration — and I'm told that I inspire the artist, the
    naturalist, the hiker, the camper, the lover, the child
    and the adult — is through my being.

I watched the waters recede, the stone man hunt, build his firepits and raise his family, leaving behind his artifacts of occupation.

I watched as the Indian hunter, traveler and displaced persons followed the streams, sought game, fished, raised and developed corn, and accepted the displaced Palatines.

I overlook the driftwood bridge from whence the County of Schoharie derived its name.

The rivalry between the Dutch and the German, the fertile valley with its wheat, hops, corn and today's great variety of agricultural developments, lie, at my feet.

I have heard the shouts and laughter of children as they swam in the Blue Hole, and skied the slopes nearby; and the rumble of the ice as it broke apart in the freshets of spring.

I shed a tear as the clouds of war — brother against brother, neighbor against neighbor, caused fortifications to be built —

And that terrible day when flames consumed the barns and homes, and all of the valley lay in complete devestation, often passes before me.

I feel the agile feet of a Tim Murphy, Boy Scouts, Girl Scouts, and the local people as they make pilgrimages to my heights, and —

Those Easter Sunrise Services when everyone praised the Almighty for the great natural beauty about them.
"All Creation sang."

Turnpikes, floods, farms, homes, schools, octagon house, orchards, the train whistles from the valley of Cobleskill as well as Middleburgh and Schoharie, game, unusual birds, a special tree or budding flower, the coming of the horse, automobiles, hang gliders and jet planes, and then, the fog generator which secured our young men by obscuring them, and the generations of people — each were unique and important. . . .

A few of the names were: Vroman, Swart, Schuyler, Livingston, Johnson, Van Wie, Bouck, Barber, Danforth, Shaul, Becker, Byrne, Bliss, Langmuir, Schaeffer, Mattice, Youmans, Bohringer, Jenks, Helijas, Lawyer, Efner, Van Houten, Mundt, Rickard, Horan, Van Dyke.

Once I was in the Town of Middleburgh. At its formation I became part of the Town of Fulton.

I became the symbol of the Schoharie County Historical Society, the name of a yearbook, and an Eastern Star Chapter — just to mention a few.

I am — Schoharie County's outstanding landmark, the symbol of what has been, is, and will be until the end of time.

I am — Mount Onistagrawa — Vromans Nose.

Helene S. Farrell, November 3, 1984

Appendix C

Preliminary List of Flora of Vroomans Nose, Middleburgh, New York

By Michael Kudish, Ph.D., Paul Smith's College, Division of Forestry, Paul Smiths, New York, 12970

Field check on June 20, 1984. Number of species observed: 98. This is a preliminary list. There are some plants that need positive identification and some that have yet to be observed.

Key to Sites:
A. North slope along old road, mostly wooded.
B. Elbow bend in road, midslope, open area.
C. Reenter woods, upper north slope and summit ridge
D. Descent south slope

TREES
Pinus strobus, E. white pine A
Pinus rigida, Pitch pine C

Tsuga canadensis, E. hemlock A C
Juniperus virginiana, E. red cedar A C
Juglans cinerea, Butternut C D
Carya ovata, Shagbark A C
Quercus rubra, N. red oak A C D
Quercus alba, White oak C
Quercus prinus, Chestnut oak C
Populus grandidentata, Big-tooth aspen B
Ostrya virginiana, Hop hornbeam A C
Prunus serotina, Blackcherry D
Cornus florida, Flowering dogwood D
Tilia americana, Basswood A D
Fraxinus americana, Whiteash A C
Ulmus americana, Elm A
Carpinus caroliniana, Hornbeam A
Rhus typhina, Staghorn sumac A C
Malus pumila, Apple A
Prunus avium, Sweet cherry A
Amelanchier laevis, Juneberry; Shadbush A
Acer rubrum, Red maple A
Acer saccharum, Sugar maple A
Fagus grandifolia, Beech A
Acer negundo, Box elder D

SHRUBS
Prunus virginiana, Choke cherry A
Hamamelis virginiana, Witch hazel A
Diervilla lonicera, Bush honeysuckle A
Viburnum acerifolium, Maple-leaved viburnum A B
Viburnum lentago, Nannyberry B
Corylus cornuta, Hazelnut B
Berberis thunbergii, Japanese barberry B
Vaccinium vacillans, Blueberry C

Vaccinium stamineum, Deerberry C
Viburnum dentatum, Arrowwood C
Gaylussacia baccata, Huckleberry C
Rhus aromatica, Fragrant sumac C D
Comptonia peregrina, Sweetfern D
Vaccinium angustifolium, Blueberry C
Vitis sp., Grape A
Cornus racemosa, Gray dogwood A C
Rhus radicans, Poison ivy D
Arctostaphylos uva-ursi, Bearberry C

FERNS
Dryopteris marginalis, Marginal shield fern A C
Polystichum acrostichoides, Christmas fern A
Athyrium filix-femina, Ladyfern A
Cystopteris fragilis, Fragile fern A
Polypodium vulgare, Polypody C
Dennstaedtia punctilobula, Hayscented fern C
Asplenium trichomanes, Maidenhair spleenwort D

MONOCOT HERBS
Uvularia sessilifolia, Bellwort A
Maianthemum canadense, Canada mayflower A C
Carex platyphylla? Wide-leaved sedge A
Hypoxis hirsuta, Yellow stargrass C
Dactylis glomerata, Orchard grass B
Festuca elatior, Fescue B
Phleum pratense, Timothy B
Deschampsia sp., Hair grass C
Anthoxanthum odoratum, Sweet vernal grass D

DICOT HERBS
Rubus odoratus, Purple-flowering raspberry A

Aster macrophyllus, Large-leaved aster A
Aster divaricatus, White woodland aster A
Solidago caesia, Blue-stemmed goldenrod A C
Actaea alba, White baneberry A
Mitella diphylla, Bishop's cap A
Circaea quadrisulcata, Enchanter's nightshade A
Prenanthes (altissima ?), Rattlesnake root A
Hieracium pratense, Yellow hawkweed A
Rubus alleghaniensis, Blackberry A
Inula helenium, Elecampan B
Hieracium aurantiacum, Orange
hawkweed; Devil's paintbrush B
Vicia cracca, Vetch B
Stellaria graminea, Stitchwort B
Ranunculus acris, Buttercup B
Plantago (major ?) Plantain B
Rubus strigosus, Red raspberry B
Galium sp. White bedstraw B
Solidago canadensis, Canada goldenrod B
Geranium maculatum, Cranesbill B
Apocynum androsaemifolium, Dogbane C
Comandra umbellata, Bastard toadflax C
Podophyllum peltatum, Mayapple C
Hypericum perforatum, St. John's wort C
Hypericum sp. St. John's wort?? D
Antennaria sp. Pussy toes C D
Fragaria virginiana, Strawberry C
Lespedeza sp. (?) Bush clover C
Melampyrum lineare, Cowwheat C
Aquilegia canadensis, Columbine C
Hieracium venosum, Rattlesnakeweed D
Thalictrum ? *Anemone*? D
Pilea pumila. Clearstem D

Hepatica triloba, Hepatica D
Eupatorium rugosum, White snakeroot   D
Veronica officinalis, Speedwell   A

MOSSES (all on summit ridge):
Polytrichum piliferum, Haircap
Polytrichum juniperinum, Haircap
Pleurozium schreberi
Leucobryum glaucum, Pincushion moss.

Appendix D

The Study of Geology in
the Schoharie Valley

By John M. Clarke, State Geologist
January 1905

In the valley of the Schoharie creek the earliest systematic study of the paleozoic rocks of this State and the
first successful attempt to classify the strata according to
their fossils were made. While Amos Eaton was endeavor-
ing to work out the order of the strata, chiefly from their
rock characters in the region adjoining the Erie canal, the
John Gebhards, father and son, were collecting fossils in
the Schoharie valley and dividing the rock masses according to differences and similarities in these organic
remains.

When the geological survey was organized in 1836,
Lieutenant Mather, charged with the work in the first
geological district which included Schoharie, sought the

assistance of John Gebhard Jr., who thus had the opportunity to verify and complete his classification.

The region is classic to the student of geology. In the brave days when Professor Eaton lectured on geology to the Legislature of New York and Govenor Dewitt Clinton collected fossils in the leisure of his executive duties, the rocks of Schoharie were a source of stimulus and inspiration which have produced fine results in the history of this science.

Yet in all its history there has not been a geologic map of the region prepared except on an insignificant scale and no adequate account of its formations and structure have heretofore been given. It is to meet this condition, to provide students of geology and paleontology with a suitable map and guide to this attractive region that I have asked Professor Grabau to prepare the work that follows.

The Schoharie valley presents a geologic section almost unequaled in this State for its completeness. It begins low in the series with the last stages of the Lower Siluric (Lorraine) and runs high into the base of the Upper Devonic; its localities are compactly assembled and easily accessible. The valley is beautiful, fertile, hospitable and well supplied with the conveniences of living. The spot is ideal for the pursuit of an intimate acquaintance with a very considerable and typical representation of New York geology.

It is believed that this work will aid and stimulate students, clarify the geologic problems which the region presents and, as it is the outcome of a careful resurvey of the region, advance our knowledge.

ABOUT THE AUTHOR

Vroomans Nose has figured prominently in the life
of scientist-historian Vincent J. Schaefer. Its summit
was often the objective of The Mohawk Valley Hiking
Club which he founded in 1929. When he began to
plan the Long Path of New York in 1931, the Nose was
a logical landmark on the route between Gilboa and
the Mohawk River. In 1942, while associated with
Nobel Prize Laureate Dr. Irving Langmuir at the
General Electric Research Laboratory, Dr. Schaefer
invented a smoke generator capable of producing
artifical fogs to screen troops, cities, and ships from
enemy bombers in the days before radar. Vroomans
Nose overlooking a natural wind tunnel – 1,000 feet
deep and 10 miles long, provided the ideal site to
photograph the government's tests. Subsequently
50,000 of these generators were built for use in World
War II. He has been active from the beginning in the
drive to preserve the Nose for future generations.